The Wisdom of Youth

Edited by Mark Richardson

Young**Writers**
First published in Great Britain in 2006 by:
Young Writers
Remus House
Coltsfoot Drive
Peterborough
PE2 9JX
Telephone: 01733 890066
Website: www.youngwriters.co.uk

All Rights Reserved

opyright ontributors

SB ISBN 1 84602 695 4

Foreword

As part of our ongoing pursuit to present a showcase of today's best up-and-coming authors, Young Writers is now proud to present *The Wisdom Of Youth,* a collection of poems written by young adults.

Few periods in life are more turbulent - or more crucial in human development than the transition from child to young adult. The struggles and trials faced daily can shape and mould our developing persona as we take a tentative step towards our early adult lives. The poems cradled within these pages reflect on decisions made, peer pressure, objects of desire along with other topics and express the thoughts, feelings and emotions of the writer. Some poems are edgy, others cheerful and some will just make you laugh!

The Wisdom Of Youth offers a selection of these poems, as the young writers within discuss a variety of subjects and also remind us of the lighter side of life. The result is a valuable and stimulating insight into the mind-set of the modern youth, and an enjoyable read for many years to come.

Contents

Ben Appleby (14)	1
Lorna Jade Forbes	2
Amy Townsend (14)	3
Levi Kane-Thorpe (12)	4
Laura Sinclair (12)	5
Sam Russell (13)	6
Adam Owen (11)	7
Darren Marshall (13)	8
Sarah Murray (14)	9
Laura Emily Hayes	10
Manraj Gill	11
Michael Bryant	12
Priya Kapur (13)	13
Laura Whittaker (16)	14
Wardah Munsoor (14)	15
Gareth Galley (14)	16
Aiswarya Sivagnanam (14)	17
Sandra Ameer	18
Emmeline Michelle Cambridge (14)	19
Naomi Hunt (13)	20
Sophia Ali	21
Jessica Miller (16)	22
Lucy Coles (13)	23
Dawn Ellis (14)	24
Loren King (13)	25
Marian Deldelian	26
Ramsha Sajjad (13)	27
Farah Ali (19)	28
Aditya Sheth (14)	30
Katy Coupland	31
Sarah Harrison (13)	32
Hana Sustkova (16)	33
Kendal Moran (16)	34
Rebecca Caroline (15)	35
Josh Rowlands (11)	36
Deborah Ayis (17)	37
Sophia Moss (13)	38
Caroline Foster (17)	40
Jack Reynolds-Wooding (13)	41
Scott Wilson (13)	42

Rianna Painter (14)	43
Sophie Blincoe-Allsop (12)	44

Downland School, Devizes
Jordan Gulvin (12)	45

Haberdashers Monmouth School for Girls, Monmouth
Hannah Taylor (18)	46

Lyndhurst House Preparatory School, London
Cassim Dawood (11)	47

Moreton Hall Preparatory School, Bury St Edmonds
Julia Makin (13)	48

Nendrum College, Comber
Emma Crawford (13)	49
Nicki Keys (12)	50
James O'Lone (13)	51
Glen Robertson (13)	52
Stephen Reid (13)	53
Craig Annett (12)	54
Kyle McLaughlin (11)	55
Lauren McNab (11)	56
Emma Morrison (11)	57
Shannon Orr (11)	58
Emma Reid (12)	59
Adrian Wray (11)	60
Christopher Smith (12)	61
Aaron Love (11)	62
Curtis Logan (12)	63
Chelsea McAleese (11)	64
Rachel McClernon (11)	65
Erin Brooks (12)	66
Toni Davidson (12)	67
Gemma Burns (11)	68
Megan Brown (12)	69
Chloe Brown (12)	70
Lynne McVeigh (11)	71
Zara McMillan (14)	72

Kirsti McAleese (13) — 73
Sophia Johnson (12) — 74
Emma Patton (13) — 75
Graeme McCracken (13) — 76
Brian Gourley (14) — 77
Remya Michael (14) — 78
Zoë Reid (14) — 79
Sarah Osborne (12) — 80
Craig Robertson (12) — 81
Ryan Mawhinney (11) — 82
Codie Nisbet (11) — 83
Megan McCready (11) — 84
Claire Stewart (12) — 85
Adam McNeilly (13) — 86
Matthew Brooks (13) — 87
Stuart Craigan (13) — 88
Nathan Heaybourne (14) — 89

St Leonard's School, St Andrews
Adam Harris (12) — 90
Jordan Hutchison (9) — 91
Richard Ward (12) — 92
Jamie Morse (10) — 93
Tabitha Gordon-Smith (10) — 94
Mary Fox Clark (10) — 95
Viveka Kymal (9) — 96
Ruth Duck (10) — 97
Elizabeth Finney (9) — 98
Holly Milne (10) — 99
Sophie McCulloch (9) — 100
Elizabeth Clark (10) — 101
Amy Mathewson (10) — 102
Katie Overend (10) — 103
Katie Simpson (9) — 104

The Canterbuy High School, Canterbury
Samiksha Gurung — 105
Lauren Braiden (12) — 106
Ashleigh Sharif (12) — 107
Harry Turner (11) — 108
Shannon Harris (12) — 109

Johanna Barrett (11)   110
Shane Scott (12)   111
Stacie Macnally (12)   112
Kimberly Boden (12)   113
Jay Bennett (11)   114
Nathan Procter (11)   115
Chloe Jackson (11)   116
Clarissa Couzins (12)   117

Woodfield Middle School, Redditch
Humera Ansari (12)   118
Jack Watton (12)   119
Raveena Haseeb (12)   120
Matthew Knight (12)   121
Stacey Cowley (11)   122
Alex Oldnall (13)   123
Abigail Dallaway (13)   124
Sam Oldnall (11)   125
Mohammed Soban (12)   126
Jordan Taylor (12)   127
Sherniece Pearson (12)   128
Raymond Stevens (11)   129
Nabeela Khan (12)   130
Stephanie Whitworth (11)   131
Gemma Grubb (12)   132
Rochelle Parchment (12)   133
Sophie Hartles (12)   134
Rimah Rafiq (12)   135
Matthew Ivory (12)   136
James Reffin, Ryan McIlravey, Casey Truman
                         & Matthew Ivory (12)   137
Sarah Taylor (11)   138
Emma Flatley (12)   139
Coral Bruton (12)   140
Francine Walters (12)   141
Paige Maoudis (12)   142
Thomas Fletcher (12)   143
Chrissie Givans (11)   144
Lauren Poole (13)   145

Jack Stevens (13)   146
Katie Spencer (13)   147

Wycombe High School for Girls, High Wycombe
Hester Phillips   148
Louisa Connolly Burnham (14)   149
Sophie Rowe & Laura Hylton (14)   150
Chevron Peters   151
Marina Smith (14)   152
Ella Blakstad (13)   153
Holly Hewlett (14)   154
Nikki Benyon   155
Femke Hyman   156
Vicky Jewell (13)   157
Leanne Robinson (14)   158
Diana Newman   159
Sanaa Aslam & Hester Phillips   160
Beth Molyneux & Katie Hart   161
Ade, Abi, Natalie & Sabine   162
Lucy West (14) & Diana Newman   163
Ella Blakstad (13) & Holly Hewlett (14)   164
Sophie Rowe, Harriet Gwilt & Laura Hylton (14)   165
Natalie Cregan   166
Katie Hart   167

The Poems

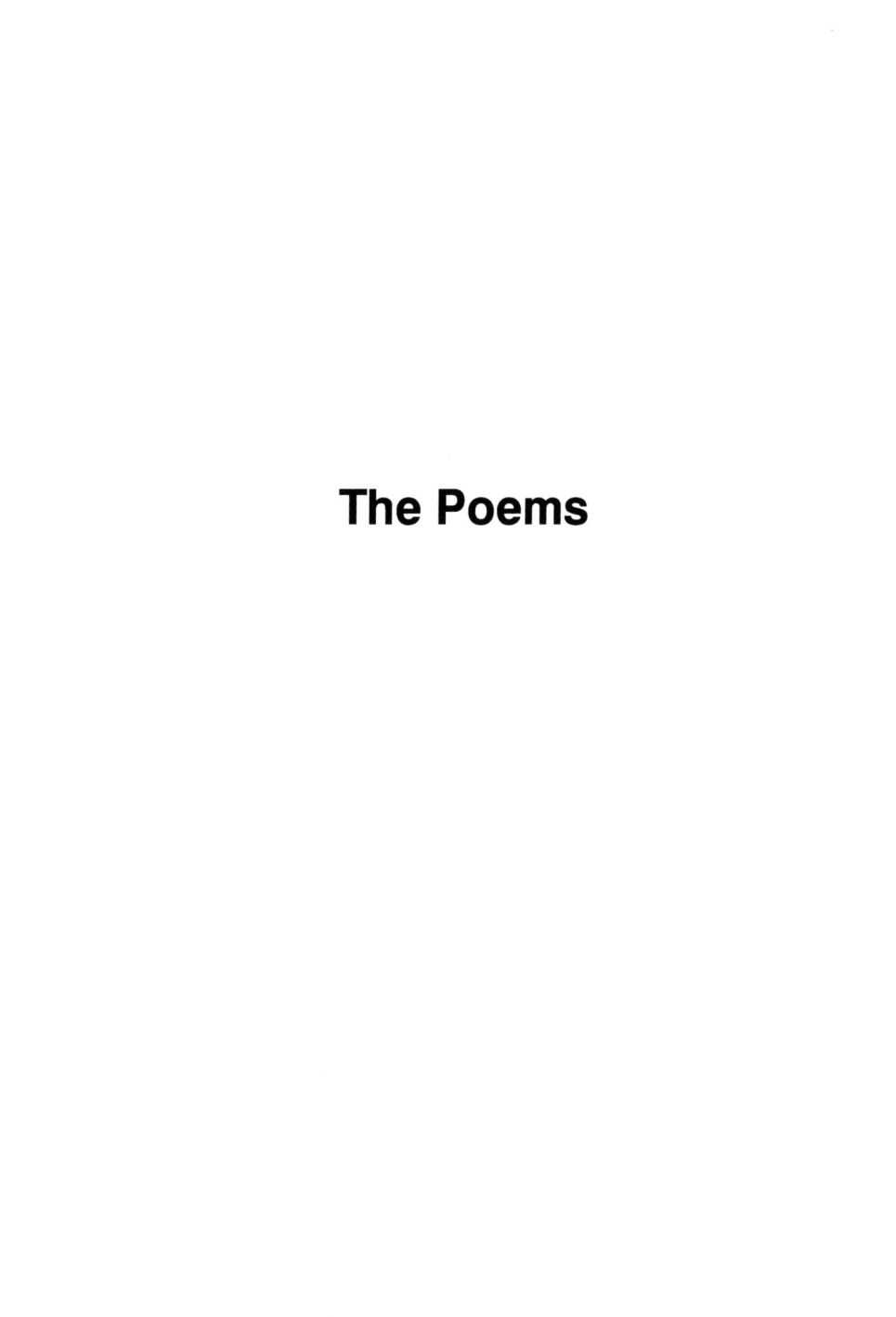

I Didn't Say Goodbye

I miss you more as time goes by,
I didn't say goodbye it feels like a crime.

I was young when you took my hand
You were the one who would understand
You calmed things down when the going got tough
Thank you for watching me from high up above.

I miss you now, I can't be mistaken
Now you're gone, my heart's still breaking
I understand that you had no choice
And I'll always remember your calming voice.

I'm sorry I didn't see you
When you hurt the most
I'm fond of these memories of me and you
Of which I have to boast.

So many things I have to ask
About your life, about your past
I'll treasure those times we had to talk
And those times we'd go on walks.

Ben Appleby (14)
Downland School, Devizes

We loved your poem Ben - so much that we chose it as the first prizewinner. You win an MP3 player! Keep up the good work.

Forever Yours

I'm not strong enough.
I'm not calm enough.
My senses have gone crazy.
This liquid is making me phase.

Your words feel like ice, piercing through my world.
I have no soul anymore.
You sucked that dry, along with my innocence.
Hurt has a new meaning with you.

I'm no good to you,
I'm no good at this.
What you needed to know,
Was in my kiss.

I love you, but it doesn't run through my veins anymore.
You love me, but it's not enough to make up for what you've said.
I'm destined to be an icy fortress, not for the faint-hearted.
Damaged goods, as you would say.

In the good times, we had some fun.
You left your mark on me, friction burn we call it.
Your touch sent thrills through my skin,
You could refill my happiness with a smile.

Can I be replenished?
Can I feel a warm touch ever again?
Do these scars run too deep?
Are we supposed to let this go, will this ever change?

Lorna Jade Forbes

> Congratulations Lorna - your poem is a prizewinner! You win £25 in book vouchers for yourself. Well done.

Destruction

I've watched you walking in the world behind my eyes;
A flower, toxic petals unfolding in my mind.
You're as cold as winter mornings and behind your killer smile
Lurks a psychopathic demon who'd like to stay awhile.

Terrorism's in your blood, the devil is your spawn -
In your eyes I see a battlefield beneath a blood-red dawn.
Your breath - contamination, corruption and decay;
You hand the kids diseases and watch them waste away.

The crimson smears upon your hands are plainer still than day,
You build houses on the meadows where the children used to play.
The animals are dying from the venom of your touch -
The all-consuming madness that you love to see so much.

The cruelty etched upon your face sends shivers down my spine,
But how dare you plant contagion on the world that once was mine?
Your sickness swift is spreading and there's little we can do,
But at least we still are trying which cannot be said for you!

Amy Townsend (14)

Well done Amy, your poem is also a prizewinner. You win a prize of £25 worth of book tokens.

Grim

Death is a thing that happens to us all,
Anyone, anywhere, anytime can die.
Some say we fall low,
Others says we fly high.

Some see a skeleton holding a scythe,
Some see a gigantic bat.
Some see their life flash before them,
Either way we all die.

Levi Kane-Thorpe (12)

A Day In The Life Of A Light Bulb

A day in the life of a light bulb
Is inordinarily tough
And I bet you'll sit there and say to this,
My job is hard enough!
But have you really thought about
What light bulbs really do?
How they work their tiny hearts out
Just to switch on and off for you.
They snap their wires and blow their fuse
Just to be there for you to use,
They burn electricity and spark off light,
Just so that they're there for you day or night.
But you still neglect them and leave them on,
So now don't you feel just a tincy bit wrong?
So next time you're sat there in that same office chair,
Give that good light bulb just a little more care.

Laura Sinclair (12)

The Mist

In a dark forest was ye,
No food, no water had he,

Nowhere to go,
Feeling low,

Walked on did he,
Passed more tree,

And only to see,
A mist did he,

The mist got lighter
And also brighter,

And only to reveal,
Something so real,

The man stood sad,
As the mist was the ghost of his dad.

Sam Russell (13)

Extraordinary Colours

Red, white, gold and blue
Who made the colours, who, who, who?

Up goes a rocket whirling and whizzing
It's so exciting, my blood is fizzing

And then there is a sound
This makes my heart pound

It is the sound of nothing
You could hear a mouse coughing

Then all of a sudden a big loud *bang!*
Like the sond of two cymbals, *clang, clang, clang!*

Then a stream of colours flood the sky
And then they die, the end is nigh.

Adam Owen (11)

What If?

I was going back to England from my holiday in Spain
When I saw strange people boarding the plane
But soon forgot and took a seat
My ears were popping, I had a sweet
As the plane took off a man stood with a gun
He pointed at a man and then his son
Then at the pilot and shot him in the head
Checked his pulse, too late he's dead
As the plane started falling out of the sky
I knew straight away I would die
The plane crashed, then I heard someone scream
But I woke up, it was only a dream
I thought to myself and then I could see
What if it really happened to me?

Darren Marshall (13)

Being A Teen

Some would say, 'It's not as bad as it seems!'
They clearly don't know what teenager means.
Others would say, 'You've got nothing to lose'
But there's embarrassing moments and subjects to choose.

There's school hierarchy and stereotypes
That channel your anger through dead-ended pipes.
Teachers constantly piling on pressure,
Nerves for exams beyond possible measure.

Senior citizens think we're all just young slobs,
But most of us are thinking of great future jobs.
There's always the occasional one who drops out,
It doesn't mean they don't know what effort's about.

All you want is to have fun with your friends,
But all of your efforts come to dead ends.
They sit and they stare; now they're picking on you.
It's not the first time it's happened, what should you do?

Sarah Murray (14)

Trevor Fights Back

The kick-off is
He hates me
Don't know why
He just hates me.
He calls me a jelly baby
And says I dress like a lady
I would never fight him,
Not cos I'm scared
It starts off when someone gets dared
I *could* beat him but I don't wanna hurt him.
The kick-off is
He thinks my legs are fat
And my long white socks are for Postman Pat
And don't get me started on my long white shorts,
My mum says they're handsome
But I don't wanna upset her
Now I'm lonesome.
But the other day, he crossed the line
He wrote 'Trevor is a cissie'
On that bag that is mine.

So I am going to fight him
Most people laugh at me and think I'm dim,
Why can't they just see me
For who I really am?

Behind the shed everyone was looking,
Smack, crack
I hit him back,
He's bleeding,
He's given up,
They all like me now!
But what about him?

Laura Emily Hayes

She

She stands, laden with jewels
Her head held low.
Her eyes linger in a daze
Searching for the answers that hold the key to her deepest desires.
Yet she stands, hoping for a sign.
A sign that leads her to a path, where there is only one route
                                          and no return.

She stands in the darkened shade of the room.
The door is closed.
The silence is deadly.
A gentle breeze touches her bare uncovered skin,
Her hands tingle and her mouth begins to tremble.
She raises her head and her eyes stare.
Awoken and alert.
The door opens.
A loud noise erupts and the silence is broken.

She stands there, laden with jewels.

The path ahead is her desire.
The route she takes is her belief.
The sign she acquires will become her inspiration.

So she walks and walks and never looks back.

Manraj Gill

Silversand Samba

Colours awaken from multi-racial flower beds,
Causing soldierly sunflowers to turn their heads,
That sleep sweet under green tree canopy ceilings,
Walled in by transcendable hologram hedges,
Paths divide, carving clean columns from the edges,
As ornate, ornamental chocolate wrappings,
Split originally coated re-arrangings.

Trees - pendular pennants percussing peacefully,
Support vines flying beyond the garden that coil,
Up from a silversand samba of shifting soil,
That moves root, stems, leaves, bushes, us - all with great toil,
Changing plants as one moves furniture so heavy,
The houses, the homes, the places that fit our keys,
Fade like the wilting leaves falling from passing trees.

Flowers rise and evolved flowers sleep in their beds,
Colours change, different every dawning,
Coated trees lose leaves like the change of clothes,
Paths expand, edges invade the beds,
The coloured flowers diverge to,
Dispersed tiny islands that,
Shrink away like melting,
Ice cream, until all,
That's left is wet,
Runny leaves
Pass on
Just
m
e
m
o
r
y.

Michael Bryant

Karma

I shall remember her face,
I shall remember the crime,
I shall remember my guilt,
I shall remember my lies.

I shall remember my beginning,
I shall remember the scene,
I shall remember that autumn,
I shall remember my fear.

I shall remember the questions,
I shall remember the sorrow,
I shall remember the day,
I shall remember the tears.

I shall remember my isolation,
I shall remember my bitterness,
I shall remember my reputation,
I shall remember those leers.

I shall remember Karma.

Priya Kapur (13)

So Perfect

I need to be perfect
I need to look like the ones on TV
I need to be the pretty girl
I need to be thin

Why aren't I perfect?
Why aren't I like them?
Why can't I be the pretty girl?
Why aren't I thin?

I try to be perfect, so I dress like everyone else
I try to be like them, so I smile all the time
I try to be the pretty girl, so I slap on loads of make-up
I try to be thin, so I starve myself each day

I'm nearly perfect now, I wear mini skirts at the age of ten
I'm nearly like them now, I get all the friends I want
I'm nearly the pretty girl now, but the make-up hurts my skin
I'm nearly thin enough now, you can see my bones through my clothes

Now I'm older, I regret being perfect, no one likes me now
Now I'm older, I regret being like them, I have a baby at fifteen
Now I'm older, I regret being the pretty girl, I got abused
Now I'm older, I regret being thin, because I nearly died.

Laura Whittaker (16)

Misunderstood

I'm never leaving my room again.
Nothing happened! Stop being nosy.
I'm not being rude. I just want to be left alone
Just *go* away!
Ground me? What've I done?
I was in a bad mood - I didn't mean to be rude.
You're not still going to ground me?
I said *please*
Please!
Alone,
Miserable
Misunderstood.

Wardah Munsoor (14)

An Excuse For Death

As the sun rises we're told to arise, to our death probably.
As the whistle blows, we lethargically scramble out of our trenches
to our death.
We walk and wait to be shot from all angles.
We see the enemy trench, our hopes soar but then you feel weak,
your body drained.
As you fall you're hit with all emotions, fear, sadness, happiness that
you're free of this nightmare called war.
You lie there and see images of your loved ones.
Hope, hope is all you have that your life may not be taken by this stupid
debate.
A dispute over nothing.
But as you lie there you realise the only way you will leave is in
a body bag.
I tell you now that there is nothing glorious about war.

Gareth Galley (14)

The Holocaust

We weep, we cry, we plead,
for us, we get no mercy; it's a done deed.
'But why?' We ask, there's no reply,
for our deaths they cannot deny.
They assumed: we had no future,
for them we were just another departure.

Have you seen the bodies row by row?
the numbers begin to grow,
have you heard of what it's like,
to be slaughtered, murdered . . . same alike?

Our lips are sealed; there will be no more speech,
for them, our lives will have a lesson to teach.
There is nothing else apart from silence,
for them, our history, shall be reliance.
'What is death?' They ask: no surprises,
for us it comes in all disguises.

Have you seen the bodies row by row
the numbers begin to grow,
have you heard of what it's like,
To be slaughtered, murdered . . . same alike?

The loss, the gain and life: we cannot retrieve,
for us, the pain we shall not relieve.
we shall never recover; the lives we gave away,
for our stories and tales, will still relay.
We laughed, we played, our lives they tore:
for we are the dead, we are no more.

Have you seen the bodies row by row,
the numbers begin to grow,
have you heard of what it's like,
to be slaughtered, murdered . . . same alike?

Aiswarya Sivagnanam (14)

Tears/Dreams

Tears
Tears are words
That the heart can say.
Sometimes we feel we can't make
It through the day
The whole world tears apart
But there's something in your heart,
That you want to say, but the
Words are getting blown away.
Remind yourself that,
There's love that falls down like rain
Let forgiveness wash away the pain.

Dreams
The best things in life are unseen
That's why we close our eyes when we dream.
Sometimes we must get hurt to grow
Sometimes we must fail in order to know.
Many people walk in and out of our lives, it seems like
Sometimes love isn't beautiful when it's burning inside
But I still have to keep my faith alive
My dreams were black and white
Until you brought colour into my life.

Sandra Ameer

Don't Let 'Em Crush Ya Dreams

Every day we get told what to do and are constantly pushed around
All of our dreams crushed, told to keep our feet on the ground
But our minds are born to dream,
If we don't have goals then how can we ever succeed?

All the teachers say, get a proper job, college then university
but I look at the life they're living and think that will never be me
I'm gonna do what I love and no force on Earth can stop me
Then all the people who doubted me will be forced to see

Dreams really can come true, and never let teachers take
                                      the dreaming out of you
'You'll never be rich, don't be silly,' is what they used to say
But let them see who's living a life of luxury each and every day

Adults may control when you go to bed and the money you have
                                                in your purse
But there's no need to let them crush your dreams because
You're in control and you can do anything
So give yourself a goal and let the dreaming begin.

Emmeline Michelle Cambridge (14)

Being A Teen - Realising

Realising that the cruel monster that lived in your dreams
                                                    was never real.

That there is worse than that in the world.
Realising that life is not a game,
Not to be played, not to be wasted.

So many questions, but so few answers,
About everything.
Religion, science, the world.
Is there life after death?
God only knows.

Space, the universe, the end of time.
What will happen in the omega?

Learning about poverty.
Children starving in complete agony.
Wishing for comfort, but not receiving.
Watching loved ones die. The evil. The emotion of it all.

Flashbacks, cherished memories, of when you were young.
Utterly oblivious about the dark reality of this world.
Man's cruel inhumanity, potential to do wrong.

War, conflict. Go back 65 years to the streets of London.
Hear the echoing of children crying and hear the screeching
                                      of bombs hitting the ground.

Your destiny and fate, lurking at the back of your mind like an
                                                unwanted memory.
Dreams from long ago, swarming your imagination like bees.

Exams, homework, school. You have to do it.
I'm enjoying every minute of it.
Only got a few years left.
Better make the most of it.
Being a teenager:
Thinking
Doing
Realising.

Naomi Hunt (13)

Good Old British Weather

Thunder, lightning and rain, the power of the thunder shakes the ground beneath me.

The rain dribbles down my window sorrowfully, leaving me nothing but insignificant leftovers.

The lightning flashes vividly. I can feel and release my own anger with the power of the torrential rain. The sound echoes through me.

It's funny how the weather can quickly turn on us. One minute we can be enjoying the happy, hot, sticky, sunny summers of joy. Then, the next minute, we will be drenched in the angry rain. To me, this day feels like we are in the Amazon rainforest, facing the monsoon climate. The goodness of the warm and welcoming weather cannot last for too long in Britain.

People are quickly rushing for shelter, some rushing into their cars, some running into shops, some trying their best to make it home safely on foot.

The homeless man and his dog are making their way to the next spot for survival, the young family are dancing their way along the street. The old couple just stand and glare from the warm indoors. Nothing and no one can control the situation.

Anyone can place a brand new building in the heart of each individual community.
Anyone can take away your possessions
Anyone can make a plane fly
But no one can take away our good old British weather.

Sophia Ali

Opposites

We live in a world of opposites.
A world of compromise.
Where morals are turned on their head.
Where nothing is wrong, yet nothing is right.

Thousands die each year,
Of diseases that are easily curable,
Yet, in the west,
We push lifespan to the limit.

And they expect us to be, oh so happy
About the prospect of space tourists
Shouldn't we sort out our own planet first?
Surely 0.7% isn't that much to spend?

We read about them in the newspapers,
Watch them on TV, hear them on the radio,
It can look so alien.
But we can turn it off, if it gets too much.

Everyone is so desperate to be famous,
Think it'll be the best,
Does anyone care anymore?
We're so self-centred.
Justice, not riches, will clean up this rotting world.

Jessica Miller (16)

Teenage Life, Good Or Bad?

Teenage life, bad or good?
The time when you leave your childhood,
Now considered older and wiser,
Other people think you are an adviser,
Friends have problems, so you help them with it,
But at your house you are in a pit,
No one to help you with problems of your own
In your room, you sit all alone.

You weep and cry but no one really cares,
You sit on your own weeping upstairs,
Your mom and dad having a row,
You sit in your room thinking how,
How is this me when my friends are happy
And when I speak, I'm always snappy!

Is it my mom and dad making me this way,
Or is it just me, I do so pray,
I hope it is not my mom or dad,
Because if they split up it will make me sad,
I will think, is it me that caused this split,
I always wanted Mom and Dad to commit.

If my mom and dad do not stay man and wife,
I must think, is this what I want for the rest of my life?
I need to act now, if I don't want to be involved,
If I decide now, my problem is solved,
No moping around, no colour black,
Always bright, and not looking back.

If I don't want to speak to someone I know,
I can always call Childline and my confidence will grow,
I can then speak to my dad and mom,
And hopefully they will not drop a bomb,
They will understand and sort themselves out,
They will then stop and think before they shout,

My life will be better and my happiness greater,
And then I'll be glad I acted now and not later.

Lucy Coles (13)

The Girl

She sat there, her life without meaning,
She felt nothing inside, no feeling,
Her blood had been withdrawn from her face,
Her heart thumping like it was a race,
Her jet-black hair flew in the moonlight,
Waiting till the moment was right,
Her dainty body, watching the riverbank,
But she couldn't think, her mind was blank,
Waiting for the next life ahead,
Through her eyes she was born dead,
She would give anything, just to get along,
Deep inside she knew she didn't belong,
She wanted to but it was too late,
But one thing was certain, death was fate.

Dawn Ellis (14)

Ice Rabbit

Sharp claws, sharp teeth,
Oh no! It's nibbling the corned beef,
Cold stare, glittering eyes,
It's very smart and very wise,
Open the door and take a peek,
Then you'll hear a tiny squeak,
Munch, munch, munch, that's all it will do,
So leave it alone, if not, it'll bite you!

Loren King (13)

Letting Go . . .

Once pastime glories are engulfed by the new
Overwhelming memories will slowly fade, to few
A box of Lego you will be given, anew,
To build the castle of your dreams

Words spoken too plainly from shivering lips:
'While change seems to loosen the strength of your grip,
It allows you to start over, your own way.'

You may wallow in grief for the lost seconds, in vain,
Or smile at the prospect of what your world may soon gain
It is time to reshape a lifetime, by day

New friends are a gift while the old are a treasure
Change may dramatise your life, yet nothing is all that lasts forever . . .
Pictures of your old built castles, proudly standing their ground,
The newest will always be the strongest, as each recent reality
                                                      is found . . .

Stack away common albums in an unforgotten attic corner,
Do not look back, or be held back, until after many years,
                                                     you remember,
That what you have left behind is what has made
                                                you grow stronger . . .

And we, in the back of your silent memory, hold the promise:
                                                 to continue to love.

Marian Deldelian

Bullying

They might be down there in the dark
Waiting for me to come down the ark
I feel the bullying tinkling through
Tell me what can I do
I fear the bullying lurking around
I can hear the footsteps sound
Why do you spread rumours about me?
Am I just invisible like a flea?
I am a human being too
I can't run and hide in the loo!
I'll beat the bully, one and all
Even if the bully is long and tall
Soon the bullies will run away . . .
And this is all I can say!

Beat bullying, beat the crime!

Ramsha Sajjad (13)

Cry Of Pain

Can you not hear my cry of pain?
I hate feeling vulnerable, weak and vain,
The world has three things,
Lies, cheats and deceit,
I carry hidden scars which cannot be seen by the naked eye,
Behind my soft laughter there is a tired sigh,
My words are my only refuge,
My sea of emotions is huge,
You have only scratched the surface, what lies beneath?
Cry me an ocean so I can drown in my tears,
I must hide my deepest fears,
I carry this heavy emotional weight,
Am I destined to this fate?
I once heard a saying, 'It's never too late',
I'll drive myself into the ground at this rate,
My past is like pieces of glass, each tells a different story,
Some reminiscent of my former glory,
I was as delicate as a rose but the wrong path I chose,
I was told it's a two-day life, you come, you go,
So what about the people who
Lied,
Cheated?
As usual, they're comfortably seated,
They get pleasure from my pain,
Life ain't a friendly game,
You win, you lose, your ego's forever bruised,
You act like you're king of your empire,
That kind of humour is satire,
My words are an illusion
Trying to figure me out will lead to confusion
I have many levels you have not seen,
I have issues but I am not mean,
Good things come to those who wait,
If you start now, it's not too late,
Between the hatred, confusion and pain,

There's a tiny light that seeps through
Reminding me to stay forever true,
Where life will take me I don't have a clue,
So this is my adios,
Goodbye, farewell, for when I see you next, only time will tell.

Farah Ali (19)

The Love Princess

From the first time my eyes did gracefully roll on her,
A fire did burn in my heart,
And a passion was born in me,
And desire given its birth.

As beautiful as an angel,
Her radiance knows no bounds.
I get lost in her charming elegance.
She is an angel rising from the ashes of the goddess of beauty

She is a goddess,
A goddess of beauty and love,
Her smile steals my heart,
Her body soft and tender
Her eyes are like two diamonds in the dark night

As graceful as a deer,
Her every motion draws my eyes to her.
Her warmth engulfs me,
And makes me reach the brink of desire.

The daughter of love,
Offspring of beauty,
Patron of love.

My inspiration,
My motivation,
The saviour of my soul
My life,
The woman who lives in Heaven.

Aditya Sheth (14)

Will It?

I just wanna tell her it's alright
Just want to say it's all OK
But I can't
Can't find the right words to say
Why?
Why can't I?
Am I stupid?
Am I dim?
No?
How can you say no?
You're not me
You're not him

I wanna wrap her up in our poorly blanket until she feels OK
She's my mother
Yes
But I wanna feel like hers
I wanna say it's OK to cry
It's OK to have that tear fall from your eye
It's not a sin
Don't hide them away
Tears are for crying
But that's all she's done today

I want her to be OK
I suppose this will just go away
I suppose one day this will all end

I know you won't understand
And I know you won't care
But I understand
I care.

Katy Coupland

I Am Amazing

I am amazing.
My hair is as strong as the same thickness of steel.
With my senses I see, I taste, I hear, smell and feel.
Inside me is enough iron for a medium-sized nail.
I contain enough water to fill five pails.

But is this all that I can be?
Is this all that makes me?

I am amazing.
I think with my mind.
It is the conscious and subconscious bind,
That keeps me together, that keeps me sane.
My mind stores the wisdom and knowledge I gain.

But is this all that I can be?
Is this all that makes me?

I am amazing.
My personality is unique.
It gives my preferences and emotional peaks.
Are we then, a set of drives?
Just a number of emotions that determine our lives?

But is this all that I can be?
Is this all that makes me?

I am amazing.
It cannot be seen, it cannot be smelt,
It cannot be heard, it cannot be felt.
The substance of my spirit is unclear to me.
But greater things it helps me to see.

But is this all that I can be?
Is this all that makes me?

Sarah Harrison (13)

Remind

Stay young, world
I will get old
So *you* will stay so
I know you

My children will be small
And you will say them
I'm small, too

Stay young world, please.

Hana Sustkova (16)

Can Angels Have Babies?
(Dedicated to Tara Preston)

Can angels have babies?
And if they could, would they be the most beautiful things ever to
                                                                    be seen?
Can an angel be a mother to an unborn child?
Can she rub her stomach, soothing the baby that will be forever
                                                                  more beguiled?
An angel shall make the best mother of all,
For her smooth wings cradle her child, acting as a wall, to protect
                                                           it from the infection of life.
Can an angel be fortified from the pain of giving birth?
Will her soothing nature soften the bitterness of the tearing between
                                                                her thighs?
Will her baby cry? Or will her comforting song silence the child's
restless lungs, carrying it to a gentle sleep?
Can an angel be disinfected from the sour tang of disease?
Or will her baby and her seize their moments together, ignorant of
                                                          the facts that befall?
An angel will make an amazing mother,
Her arms wrapping her child, keeping it warm as its rosy cheeks form,
and it slowly opens its eyes, and sighs, like an angel.
Can a baby of an angel distinguish between its first word and its
                                                                   first song?
Will it grow like its mother? Strong, yet innocent, pale yet colourful,
                                                             bold yet elegant?
Can an angel have a baby? I don't think so.
Yet a pregnant angel stands to correct me.
An angel, so maternal, so natural, she knows what she's doing.
This angel will go through the birth of her child, to later hold, this baby
to mould, into an angel like herself, with a soft glare and long, strong
ribboned hair, a beautiful baby, requested by a prayer.
Can angels have babies?
Yes, I guess they do.
This angel of mine has proven to me it's true.
An angel's baby can grow with its wings. Fasten her halo, giggles
                                                                     and sings.
And her mother's sweet song will always send her to sleep.
An angel's baby is forever hers to keep.

Kendal Moran (16)

All Things Real

She does it on purpose.
She enjoys the feeling of pain.
It's normal to her; it's become a routine.
Nobody understands her; they say she's insane.

They don't know about it,
She never lets it show.
Outside she looks well
But inside they don't know.

The blades become her friend,
Her scars will never heal.
She's killing herself slowly and she knows it.
The scars are a souvenir of all things real.

Only one thing can save her,
The voice she longs to hear.
Stopping instantly as there is a reason to live,
Falling down her cheek is a tear.

She's too late at stopping,
The blood keeps pouring out.
With her last breath she says sorry,
Another life gone out.

Rebecca Caroline (15)

Untitled

I never knew this would come to pass,
the day I got sent over the top
I knew my life would not last.
I keep my letters close to my heart
and read them every day.
If I could see one of my children
then it would make my day.
My friend's been sent to no-man's-land
to die a certain death.
I only wish I could have seen him before his last breath.
Now that he has gone,
I can't stand this pain.
I'm going to end this war
by putting a bullet through my brain.

Josh Rowlands (11)

My Puzzle

I feel my life drifting
I know I am slipping
When I am feeling like dipping
My heart, my soul is ripping
I can feel my blood rippling
I jump off my tree limb
Cos now I am tripping
That no one is killing
My life is spinning
And I am in the middle
It's like a long riddle
I just can't wait to solve the puzzle
Yesterday I was facing the muzzle of a gun
But today I see people nuzzle
While they are eating pizza
I don't know why I am still sizzling
When I can feel the rain of joy drizzling.

Deborah Ayis (17)

Broken Doll

Hit her and she will fall,
She ain't alive so she can't crawl,
See her break and turn away
Like you did yesterday,
Brush right past her,
Don't look back,
You don't care
Your life's on track,
Stand on a piece of her
And you don't even notice.

She is a broken doll,
She's lost a piece of her soul,
She'll come back together,
But she will leave behind
A piece of her
That she can't find,
Broken doll . . .

She gets broken every single day,
You would think by now she wouldn't care what people say
But she cries broken tears still.
Her looks have gone after all these years,
She's been abandoned for so long
And you don't even think it is wrong
To just break her and don't look back to see.

Doll, how did you turn so wrong?
Why did this become such a sad song?
Why do people just brush by?
Don't they see the way you cry?
Does no one put you back on the shelf?
Does nobody care?
Why can't someone buy you?
Why can't there be nice people somewhere?

When you look in shop windows
You may see her there,
You may walk past her
Or you may stop and stare,
But you wouldn't go in and buy her,
You wouldn't hug and hold her,
You don't care.

Sophia Moss (13)

Phoenix

Pure gold feathers, downy soft.
Graceful neck, head held aloft.
Hazel eyes, which radiate warmth.
Her crimson wings take flight,
Behold the phoenix of the light.

And yet, despite
Those joyous rays,
A dark shade must descend
And bring this good light to an end:

Silver feathers, steely blades.
Mysterious cool, seen through a glaze.
Emerald eyes, like gleaming stones.
Her shadowed wings take flight,
Beware the phoenix of the night.

Caroline Foster (17)

A Night On The Street

I remember a night on the street
All the people that come and peep
I remember a night on the street
Trying to gather a load of paper so I could lay and sleep
I remember a night on the street
When I couldn't feel a thing from hands to feet
I remember a night on the street
When it's black and bitter and I start to weep
And all I can hear
Is people coming by and stamping their feet
I remember that night on the street.

Jack Reynolds-Wooding (13)

The Girl That Turned Into A Tree

She entered the park
And was walking her dog.
When she soon felt tired
And sat down on a log.

That was when it happened,
When she changed her mood,
Her young fleshy body
Was turned into wood.

She couldn't get up
And neither could her dog.
Her clothes were ripped off
As she became part of the log.

Her hair became leaves
And her face became hidden.
Her ears became holes
For animals to put things in.

Now she stands there
As a cold dead tree,
Wishing she was human
Like you and like me.

Scott Wilson (13)

Where Is The Justice?

As the phantom blows the wind up the beach,
It brings sadness and woe.
Grains of happiness that have been
Diminished by the powers that be.

All hope is lost,
Even the sour tears are drying up.
Times have passed,
It is too late.

Hopes shattered,
Ambitions destroyed.
The reason?
Selfishness.

One person wanting all for himself,
Careless,
His eyes blind to the suffering,
He only considers *his* dreams.

Buried in lies,
They wait each day,
Wait for their lives to begin.
They surely have not yet begun.

Maybe they have?
From birth it was inevitable,
An innocent child sentenced to a lifetime of suffering.
Where is the justice?

There isn't any here.

Rianna Painter (14)

The Alley Cat

In the darkness
It slinks by
The creature and its artfulness.

Prowling and growling
It catches a mouse.
The mouse squeaks in panic,
The cat goes manic.

It gobbles it down
Without a sound.
That was only a snack
For a very hungry *cat*!

Sophie Blincoe-Allsop (12)

What Did I Achieve In Life?

I have nothing in hatred, just lonely all day,
I have nothing to do with hatred as I cry on the bay.
I am wondering; what did I achieve in life?
Just the same sad loser, I always was in strife.
How could I be so stupid to think I would make friends.
But the thing is, the morbidness never ends,
I keep thinking things will get better,
No, in fact it always gets worse.
I think of all the things in life
That always make me sad.
Just a lonely old boy in the world
Frightened of his own shadow.

Jordan Gulvin (12)
Downland School, Devizes

Butterfly

She flapped her near-exhausted wings in the fanning of a
                                                  midnight breeze,
And all at once a pain she met that brought her swirling to her
                                                  insect knees.
A fluttering of life that once lifted hopes of all,
Now lying dead and crushed - bruised against some broken
                                                  garden wall.
Her dreams were flighty in her day-old head,
A nettle in the sun with leaves upon which her infant young son
                                                  could feed -
This food is fit for admirals and peacocks yet some would call it weed.
Broken dreams lie now in sultry shaded flakes among abandoned
                                                  hoes and rakes,
She cannot be a dreamer anymore.
Vision and hopes of swarms of glittering wings all of her kind
                                                  are filling up
The dying breaths and memoirs of her tiring mind.
There were so many things she meant to do before she went,
So many things - and none of them were these grim parodies of
                                                  martyred deaths,
Hers were not the greatest aspirations, or do not seem that way to us,
Simple moonlit assignations filling time with firefly lit flapping in
                                                  the endless
Fairy-light sky - now she starts to wonder why it had to end so soon.
No one will remember she existed by tomorrow's lazy summer
                                                  afternoon -
Except the little girl might say, 'Where is the butterfly today?'
Expired exotic winged thing, now the Earth will now accept you in,
For what is gone shall grow again in death to feed the growing,
The nettles lie behind her, and their seeking roots shall find her -
Let her hopes take flight in the clouds of nameless children
Which will fill the summer's autumn air.

Hannah Taylor (18)
Haberdashers Monmouth School for Girls, Monmouth

Cheetah

Fast as a dart
goes with a start.
Hunts his prey
like a stingray.

Waits in the grass,
will his prey pass?
The herd of buffalo
while he lays low.

Then he dives
to kill some lives.
He attacks with all his might,
he has a feast tonight.

Cassim Dawood (11)
Lyndhurst House Preparatory School, London

The Lemon

Many are fooled by my appearance,
In a perfect oval shape,
Tiny grooves lie in my tough skin.
A beauty am I, with my colour
Brightest yellow, a picture for any artist
To paint. Cut me open to find the juiciest
Of all juices, packed to perfection in
Tiny, pale droplet cups.

Such a perfect look. Surely the taste
Of this fruit will be sweeter than the sweetest,
More mellow than ever tasted before?
But ah! My victims have judged by my appearance!
Bite into me and taste a terrible flavour,
It's sourness no man can find, a fruit that can beat.
In my heart my colour is harsh and black,
My feel cold and sharp. I have tricked you as
I have tricked many others.

No, I am not an angel's fruit, but a creature like
The Devil, waiting to strike under an angel skin.

Julia Makin (13)
Moreton Hall Preparatory School, Bury St Edmonds

Noise

Noise, I like noise,
The crashing and bashing of a stormy night,
The click of a switch as you turn on the light,
The clicking of shoes as they walk up the road,
The gentle croaking of a toad,
The buzzing bees flying around,
A cat purring, what a gentle sound,
Children laughing as they play,
A gentle breeze on a summer's day,
Fireworks whizzing through the sky,
Rustling bags full of things you buy,
Money jingling in your pocket,
The gentle click as you open a locket,
Noise, I like noise.

Emma Crawford (13)
Nendrum College, Comber

Noise!

Noise, noise, noise, I like noise,
The banging of drums, the popcorn that pops,
High heels that go clip-clop.
The whistling of the kettle, the squeaking of the chair,
The snipping and snipping of my long hair.
The ticking of the clock, the bubbling of the bath tub,
The growls from a young cub.
The turning of a key, the hissing of the frying pan,
The vibrating of the fan.
Noise, noise, noise, I like noise!

Nicki Keys (12)
Nendrum College, Comber

Noise

I like noise!

The squeak of a guinea pig, the miaow of a cat,
The yelp you hear when you step on a rat.
The beating of music, the click of a pen,
The beautiful tweet of a chitty wren.

The gushing of water, the bang of the bands,
The slosh of water as it splashes the sand.
The roar of a lawnmower, the rushing of traffic,
The tingling sound when you pull on elastic.

The click of clogs, the splat of an orange,
The squeaky sound of a rusty door hinge.
The sound of a blender, the smashing of glass,
The whirr of a strimmer as it cuts the grass!

James O'Lone (13)
Nendrum College, Comber

I Like Noise

I like noise,
The popping of popcorn, the drill in the pit stop,
The sound of a car horn,
The sound of music like rock and pop,
The ripping sound of paper being torn.

The shatter of a window, the chant of a footy crowd,
A screech of a car, the car engine getting really loud,
The sound of the car when the accelerator is floored,
The swishing, slashing sound of a general's sword.

Glen Robertson (13)
Nendrum College, Comber

Noise

I like noise,
The ring of a bell, the horn of a car,
The ding-dong of a clock that reaches the hour,
The screech of a firework, the thud of a drum,
The sound of me devouring a big purple plum.

The stamping of feet, the clash of the lid of a bin,
The rustle of leaves blowing in the wind,
The singing of birds, the sound of pelting rain,
The sound of really bad pain.

Stephen Reid (13)
Nendrum College, Comber

Hallowe'en

H aunting creatures stalk the night
A ll the little kids in sight
L it candles shining very bright
L anterns and costumes filled with fright
O range pumpkins large and round
W itches can be seen with their black cats flying off the ground
E veryone can hear creepy sounds
E veryone watches the fireworks as they whizz round and round
N ow the night has gone and the day has dawned.

Craig Annett (12)
Nendrum College, Comber

Me Kennings

Love food,
Good mood.

Cat scarer,
Grudge bearer.

Olive hater,
Not a skater.

Sweet spender,
Money defender.

Biscuit muncher,
Sweet cruncher.

Big smile,
That's Kyle.

Kyle McLaughlin (11)
Nendrum College, Comber

Me Kennings

Love dogs,
Hate frogs,
Chocolate hater,
Rabbit taker,
Money spender,
Sweetie lender,
Brother hater,
Crazy eater,
Ice skater,
Ballet hater.

Lauren McNab (11)
Nendrum College, Comber

Me Kennings

Cat lover,
Hate brother,
Sweet sharer,
Ice hockey player,
Dog carer,
Teddy bear,
Love to cuddle,
What a muddle.

Emma Morrison (11)
Nendrum College, Comber

Me Kennings

Dog lover,
Boy hugger.

Money spender,
Sweet lender.

Hamster hater,
Teddy beater.

Netball player,
Bad starer.

I'm a bore,
I'm Shannon Orr.

Shannon Orr (11)
Nendrum College, Comber

Recipe For Happiness

A cupful of playing my pipes,
A teaspoon of TV,
A slice of eating sweets,
A jug full of going to Newcastle,
A touch of hanging about with my friends,
A spoonful of playing my PlayStation,
An ounce of netball
And a scoop of ice cream and jelly!

Emma Reid (12)
Nendrum College, Comber

I Am

I am a scientist making
And mixing chemicals.

I am a builder knocking down
And building houses and buildings.

I am Adrian Wray in 8K,
Good at English, bad at maths.

Adrian Wray (11)
Nendrum College, Comber

Me Kennings

Bad thinker,
Fanta drinker,
Mad hatter,
Girl catcher,
Window watcher,
Greedy snatcher,
Spider killer,
Cat filler,
Dog lover,
Big brother.

Christopher Smith (12)
Nendrum College, Comber

Recipe For Happiness

A slice of playing the Xbox,
Pour in playing with my friends,
An ounce of playing with my dogs,
Add a pinch of listening to my music,
Mix with some football and rugby,
Stir in chilling in my room,
Bake with a little kick boxing,
Then serve with a lot of golf
And now the recipe's done.

Aaron Love (11)
Nendrum College, Comber

Me Kennings

BMX jumper,
Crisp muncher,
Stuff maker,
Rain hater,
Simpsons rule,
Cats drool,
Football despiser,
BMX trier,
Trick player,
Sweet sharer,
Snow lover,
TV hugger,
Internet surfer,
Red Bull perker,
I'm a he,
That's me.

Curtis Logan (12)
Nendrum College, Comber

I Am

I am Mariah Carey singing to the crowd,
Being the best singer in the world,
The crowd cheering me on and waving their hands.

I am a spy, spying on people, being the best spy in the world,
The only spy in the world and the best.

I am a model, being the prettiest all the time
And winning all the time too.

I am Chelsea McAleese, in 8K at Nendrum College,
I'm good at English and maths,
I like art because I like drawing and painting
And I like H.E because I like cooking and making.

Chelsea McAleese (11)
Nendrum College, Comber

Me Kennings

I am a . . .
Chocolate lover,
Dog hugger.
Crazy skater,
Fashion traitor.
Dough spender,
Great mender.
Boy crazy,
I'm lazy.
Sweet muncher,
Crisp cruncher.
Money stealer,
I'm a leader.
Daydreamer,
Not a screamer.
I'm a she,
That's me!

Rachel McClernon (11)
Nendrum College, Comber

Me Kennings

I am a
TV liker,
Speedy biker,
Boy thinker,
Cola drinker,
Hate bats,
Love cats,
Sweet muncher,
Crisp cruncher,
Come run,
Love fun,
Good looks,
Erin Brooks.

Erin Brooks (12)
Nendrum College, Comber

Me Kennings

I am a . . .

Make-up wearer,
Sweet sharer.

Cat hater,
Dogs later.

Sweet cruncher,
Biscuit muncher.

Not a biker,
Football liker.

Crazy hunter,
Not a punter.

Who is she?
Mean me.

Toni Davidson (12)
Nendrum College, Comber

My Recipe For Happiness

Four ounces of dancing, ballet mostly,
A jug full of boys,
A ladle full of making Scoobies,
A pinch of TV,
A kettle full of my family,
A bottle full of hanging around with my mates,
A sprinkle full of clothes,
One ounce of singing.

Gemma Burns (11)
Nendrum College, Comber

Me Kennings

Loud singer,
Boy ringer.

Shop to dropper,
Sock lender.

Make-up wearer,
Sweet sharer.

Crazy dancer,
Bit of a chancer.

Book hater,
Not a skater.

Crown lover,
It's me, Megan Brown.

Megan Brown (12)
Nendrum College, Comber

I Am

I am Mary King, horse riding and jumping through
the cross country course, faster and faster they go,
when they stop they stop.

I am a policewoman, fighting and catching criminals and baddies,
they lock them up
and you will never ever see them again.

I am a piece of money, taking me to shops
and spending the money (which is me)
on sweets and other goods.

I am Chloe Brown, 8K, good and bad at maths
but I am also OK at art and English.

Chloe Brown (12)
Nendrum College, Comber

Hallowe'en

H aunted house on a hill
A s dark as a night, there is no one in
L ittle children go trick or treating
L ittle children are scared and go off weeping
O ut and about there are bats
W itches are back and they smell like rats
E ating apples and apple pies
E ating nuts and dressing up
N ights are dark and they will give you a fright.

Lynne McVeigh (11)
Nendrum College, Comber

A Little Tiny Baby

A bundle of joy
A bundle of laughs
A little tiny baby
To hold in your arms
With little tiny fingers
And little tiny toes
Little tiny hands
And a little tiny nose.

A squeal and a cry from baby
Mummy goes
To feed the little baby
Before a long doze
It's up to the nursery
And into the cot
All snug and warm
The baby sleeps.

The noise of tiny feet running around the floor
As you try to dress baby before going out the door
Out you go and around the block
Squeaks of joy from baby
As you walk around the block once more.

The end of the day comes
With baby sleeping in the cot
And Mummy in her bed
Both dreaming of what tomorrow will bring
A walk in the park perhaps or a trip to the sea
I don't know, you'll just have to wait and see.

Zara McMillan (14)
Nendrum College, Comber

Happy Christmas

Happy Christmas
And a happy New Year.
People getting their presents wrapped
And ready to give to other people.
People sharing their homes with family,
You should all be grateful, especially at this time of the year.
Children looking out for Santa coming,
Hoping they get what they wanted.
Ready for the day coming,
It's very exciting for them.
Santa has been and gone by the time they wake up.
The gifts are wrapped and under the tree,
Many got the toys they wanted
As well as other presents.
Soon as it's over, it all happens again.

Kirsti McAleese (13)
Nendrum College, Comber

Christmas

Christmas,
It is a time for
Families to come
Together and a time
When children get loads
Of presents under the tree,
Children play all day and enjoy
The snow and fun, they play with their
Friends and they play with every toy.
So get shopping and enjoy the fun.
Night-night
Go straight
To sleep 'cause
Santa's on his way.

Sophia Johnson (12)
Nendrum College, Comber

Christmas

M erry Christmas
E veryone happy and having a good time
R unning up to see what Santa has got them
R ight away the smiles are on their faces
Y ou're so happy to see them smile.

C hristmas has come, and the countdown has begun
H appy Christmas to all
R eady for the day to come
I cing on the Christmas cake
S anta has been
T he time will come for him to come again
M any got the toys that they wished for
A s well as the things that they wanted
S oon it will be over and it will happen again.

Emma Patton (13)
Nendrum College, Comber

Heatwave

Literally sweating a pool,
I lay on a liquid dripping deckchair.
Burnt to a cinder by the scorching sun
Tyres stick to the road.
Red-faced children at a halt,
Car fumes roasting away.
As you dozed in the sun
Skin turns deep red.
Everytime you move or stretch
You feel your bone dry clothes
Crinkle like a crisp.
Lying in that deckchair
Still sweating a pool.

Graeme McCracken (13)
Nendrum College, Comber

Our Park

Our park, our park
Where all the children play,
Swinging on the cold metal swing chains,
Getting higher, then higher
Until you get goosebumps.
Then to the monkeybars,
We climb over and under,
Then side to side
On cold steel bars.
Head to the playing fields
With the beautiful green grass,
Where we play football
And roll in dirt.

Brian Gourley (14)
Nendrum College, Comber

The Park

The park in the middle of a city
The wind humming in the ears
And passing away
The sun shaded
At the dawn
Birds are singing
Heavy rush in the park
Cars crawl by
The park in the middle of a city
Red-faced children playing
Dry ground
Ice-blue sky
Heatwave drives swings
Sweating people
Come to the shade of the trees
The sun drowsing in the west
Darkness falls
Birds sleeping in trees
Liquid dripping, lights on
The side of the roads
The park in the middle of the city.

Remya Michael (14)
Nendrum College, Comber

Heatwave In The City

Heatwave in the city
Red-faced children in pushchairs
People in the shade, stretched out dozing
Lazing under the trees
Deckchairs, ice-blue sky
Lazy days, humming bees
Fair-haired children in deckchairs drowsing
Through the gates colourful cars crawl by
Earth, dry, cracking, cracking
Red-faced children dripping sweat
On hot metal swings
Heatwave in the city.

Zoë Reid (14)
Nendrum College, Comber

I Am

I am a reporter reading out news,
Sitting at my desk reading what I need to say.

I am a hairdresser doing people's hair,
Cutting and colouring hair, sometimes making tea or coffee.

I am teacher teaching away,
Doing English, never stop teaching away.

I am Sarah Osborne. I am OK at cooking
But not great, I like maths but hate English.

Sarah Osborne (12)
Nendrum College, Comber

Recipe For Happiness

A slice of cuddling with the dog,
Stir and add a fun day with your brother and sister.
Wait for ten minutes,
Add a splash of money from your mum,
Stir well; put in a pinch of your granny.
Throw in a piece of chicken and mix well,
Add the love from your family.
Serve with crackers and cheese.

Craig Robertson (12)
Nendrum College, Comber

Me Kennings

I am a . . .
Cola drinker,
Bad thinker,
TV watcher,
Girl catcher,
Food eater,
Football hater.

Ryan Mawhinney (11)
Nendrum College, Comber

I Am

I am a vet, helping animals all around, giving a helping hand,
A vet is always there to help.

I am a dog trainer, giving them jobs such as:
A guide dog, a guard dog, or maybe just a pet.

I am a fashion designer, designing tops, trousers,
Jackets, dresses and shoes.

I am a beauty stylist, styling hair, doing nails, waxing eyebrows
And doing relaxing massages.

I am Codie Nisbet, rubbish at maths and good at English.

Codie Nisbet (11)
Nendrum College, Comber

I Am

I am a fairy gliding through the air sending joy everywhere.
I am a horseback rider racing through the fields.
I am a stunt car racer doing stunts.
I am a mechanic working on cars.
I am an animal minder minding animals when people are on holiday.
I am Megan McCready in 8P, I must stop talking in class.

Megan McCready (11)
Nendrum College, Comber

My Recipe For Happiness

My ingredients and measuring are . . .
A splash of lazing around in the pool.
A cup of raging on a Saturday night.
A large tablespoon of tickling the dog.
A slice of disco dancing.
An ounce of TV.
A splash of summer sun baking.
A pinch of messing around.
Sprinkle with a couple of beautiful barbecues.
Pour in my oldest and my favourite jeans,
And a good helping of family fun.
An ounce of karaoke.
An ounce of playing football.
Mix up well
With a splash of playing on my laptop
And a large tablespoon of listening to music
And half a cup of making Scoobies.
Pour in my favourite buzzbroad
And a handful of money to spend on clothes.
Stir in my favourite T-shirt
And my cute cousin.
Serve with my adorable niece
And there you go, my recipe is done.

Claire Stewart (12)
Nendrum College, Comber

Dermott Road At Night

Depressing, lonely, surrounded by houses,
The glow of orange street lights flickering away,
Fireworks swooshing and the moon glowing like a crystal ball!
The glowing of TVs in houses glowing against the wall.
Twinkling stars and a painted black sky!
Not a person or a shadow to be seen!
Lingering fog falling, musky smoke coming from chimneys,
Littered with leaves, some green, some orange!
Gentle wind blows the leaves tumbling along with a crunch!

Adam McNeilly (13)
Nendrum College, Comber

Ice Bowl Disco

Dancers' heaven, ravers' circle, laser paradise
Beats beating, music blasting
DJs mixing their magical beats
Flashing lights blazing down
Lasers attack from every angle
Dancers dancing and will not stop.

Matthew Brooks (13)
Nendrum College, Comber

Christmas Lights

Winter's cold, white and bare
The constant twinkle of many a star
The striking white snow sitting dormant
The laughter and joy of people receiving presents
Clatter of knives and forks hitting plates
The warmth within every house
Cars covered with snow that can't be seen anymore
The heaped presents beneath the Christmas tree
And still the snow falls.

Stuart Craigan (13)
Nendrum College, Comber

My Nanas And Papas

Skies like holy lights, fruit like the rainbow,
Big burning, hot round ball of fire.

The flowers open up one by one,
Opening for the bright warm sun.

When the sun comes out to stay,
All the clouds drift away.
Birds chirp many jolly, cheerful songs,
Sadly they don't sing all day long.

Nathan Heaybourne (14)
Nendrum College, Comber

Bird's View

Brown line,
White froth
Tinkles through the river trough.
By and by the birds fly over the riverside carved by time.
Further and further over the green-leafed trees,
Plastered by the blossom
Picked by the bees.

Adam Harris (12)
St Leonard's School, St Andrews

The Leaf Of Life

The leaf of life
Has lived for many years
And he still lives.
It is so quiet.
It is the only leaf I have talked to,
It may be the only leaf I know . . .
The new leaf
Has been born
And new with life
And will live forever and ever.

Jordan Hutchison (9)
St Leonard's School, St Andrews

An Iguana's Landscape

Long tail, long tongue, bright green,
And I have a frilly neck.
Tropical warm weather with steam creeping up branches
High in the air.
Vines crawling on the ground below.
Drops of water shimmer.
Delicate flowers tremble as I climb past.
It is a kingdom of juicy bugs.

There is a strange barrier you cannot see,
And beyond is a cold grey world.
There are strange animals there,
Some have four round black legs
And they eat those other animals,
The ones with two long legs.

Look! Those two legged animals are here.
They stare at me,
Point with weird stubby claws.
The smallest has a square black insect,
An insect with a long round nose
That moves in and out.

Click!
'Hey look I got a picture of the iguana.'
What, I think, is an iguana?
But they are leaving already,
Past that sign saying,
Welcome to Stratford Butterfly Farm.

Richard Ward (12)
St Leonard's School, St Andrews

The Pictures Of The Sky

Early in the morning if you look out
You will see the sky explode
Into the pictures of your dreams
The red hills of the fire that melts the ice
Of the Arctic lakes
That cause the green waterfalls to turn into the swivelling river
That feed the mythic trees
That continues to the endless desert of the dried oasis.

Jamie Morse (10)
St Leonard's School, St Andrews

I'm Just A Tree, Humans Don't Bother About Me

I'm crumbling with old age standing right next to the roaring
Not blue, but murky green sea,
Humans don't bother about me.

They let me fall apart,
My leaves crumble and drift away
Into the murky green sea.

Wait,
What do I see?
It's campers,
I hope they are going to camp by me.
No! Don't snap, crash
And bang into me.
Too late . . .
Now look at what's left of me.

I'm just a stump of an old oak tree,
I wish humans hadn't bothered about me!

Tabitha Gordon-Smith (10)
St Leonard's School, St Andrews

Never-Ending

Rushing rivers racing past,
Purple mountain, standing tall, straight and high,
Chocolate waterfalls making gurgling noises,
Flowery fields stretching on and on to the pink horizon.

Gripping grass going on and on,
Twirling trees waving about,
Marvellous meadows making grain,
Sweet streams whizzing by.

And to me it's never-ending beauty.

Mary Fox Clark (10)
St Leonard's School, St Andrews

The Wild Elephant

Dark the forest trees
With shadows stretched along the ground.
The sun bright in the sky
Like an arched rainbow
In red, green, purple and blue,
The colourful Indian birds fly
Merrily chirping a sweet song.
The thunder of an elephant's feet breaking the hushed silence
Staring with his big, bulgy, beautiful eyes,
The trumpeting scream of his angry cry,
His tusks as sharp as a knife and as white as icicles.
The trees bow behind him as flat as a pancake,
The grass bent and yellow under his filthy fat feet.
Everything still,
All that is there is the elephant with Indian trees,
Some trampled, some still standing,
There with yellow and green grass by its side,
Indian birds still chirping away
All in the Indian jungle.

Viveka Kymal (9)
St Leonard's School, St Andrews

Angry

Mountains huge,
So high they go through the sky.
White clouds that cannot be seen
By the eagles hovering by.
Not cosy green,
Black hills, curling round the mountain.

Sea, misty black
Not turquoise,
Sun bright but sad
In the dead blue sky.
Angry afternoon.

Sun bright orange
Not gloomy grey.
Grass cosy green.
Trees have leaves.
Good-humoured afternoon.

Ruth Duck (10)
St Leonard's School, St Andrews

Landscape

Proudly the trees stand high
Mountains look above the clouds

Into the darkness of space

The grass is like beautiful silk
Soft and smooth

While streams make a lullaby sound
With water clear, fresh and cool

The sea takes the reflection of the sun
Down into the wet blue water.

Elizabeth Finney (9)
St Leonard's School, St Andrews

My Imaginary Landscape

Marshmallow soft,
Moody milk meadows.
Mushy mud,
Melted marshmallows all runny and soft.
Creamy candyfloss for clouds,
Incredible icing for the frost,
Small Smartie-like pebbles in the stream.
Gorgeous golden syrup sun
In my imaginary landscape.

Holly Milne (10)
St Leonard's School, St Andrews

The Sparkling Stream

The water trickles down the stream,
Nothing gets in her way
As she hurries down to the sea.
Sparkly water just good enough to drink,
She shines in the light
But paddling people
Make ripping rapids.
But no matter how many ripping rapids they make
She is still going strong.

Sophie McCulloch (9)
St Leonard's School, St Andrews

Australia

Yellow mountains shimmer in the sun
Shining bright for all to see,
With great brown kangaroos bouncing in the mist,
Little joeys in their pouches.
The sparkling rain like sharks' teeth with the white sun
Shining in the sky with all the blue heather and colourful hills,
Only in Australia.

White snowy mountains like crystal
That shimmers in the sun so crunchy and hard,
All the birds soaring in the bright blue sky,
Skiing in the soft white snow.
Deer pouncing in the bright green grass,
Only in Scotland.

Elizabeth Clark (10)
St Leonard's School, St Andrews

Landscape

The landscape is like a cape around the land,
Keeping it safe from warriors in space,
That float on red clouds holding a bow and arrow.

Us human beings are protected by the land's cape.
The land may be flat, the land may be sloped,
But it is our cape.

Amy Mathewson (10)
St Leonard's School, St Andrews

Desert Tree

I sit with the sand blowing in my face
Looking out at the everlasting flatness
Of the desert.

People lying, panting and sweating,
Pulling at my rough date-hair, leaning against my trunk,
I feel the sand of the desert.

People shout with relief as they reach me,
I am their saviour,
They know water and safety are near,
I hear the sound of the desert.

I smell the candyfloss clouds gently passing over,
I smell the sun and the rain will draw near,
I smell the skies of the desert.

I taste the sand blowing in my face,
The moon and the stars taste of the night,
I taste the clear night skies of the desert.

The senses of the desert,
If only I could be a bird
But I am only a date palm
Trying to survive.

Katie Overend (10)
St Leonard's School, St Andrews

Sparkling Summer

The fields of grass,
Luscious and green.
The sky as blue,
As blue as can be.
Trees and bushes
Whistle through
The breeze,
Talking in their
Whispering way.
Birds singing
Their merry tune,
All is happy,
Out comes the moon.

Then to rest
Sleepy heads,
Snuggling up
In cosy beds.
In morn they
Shall rise,
Going to
The land
Of everlasting blue skies.

Katie Simpson (9)
St Leonard's School, St Andrews

Daffodils

Springtime has come, springtime has come,
Daffodils are on the ground,
Yellow and bright like the sun,
Makes you cheerful all day and all night.

Springtime has come, springtime has come,
Daffodils are on the ground,
As scented as a perfume counter,
Makes bees wander and wonder.

Springtime has come, springtime has come,
Daffodils are on the ground,
Smooth and soft curving around,
Makes my mum want to buy one.

Samiksha Gurung
The Canterbuy High School, Canterbury

To Be Human

To be human is to love somebody,
Not to be human is to love yourself and no one else.
To be human is to look after your parents,
Not to be human is to not care about others.
To be human is to love McFly's Danny Jones!
Not to be human is just to love yourself!

Lauren Braiden (12)
The Canterbuy High School, Canterbury

The Magic Box
(Based on 'Magic Box' by Kit Wright)

In the box I have . . .

Sparkling sand in the sun
Waves crashing as they come
Lots of dogs chasing their tails
All the rest are ripping mail

In my box I have . . .

Creamy candy walls
With lots of chocolate balls
My floor is soft like cotton wool
My box is warm but yet so cool

In my box I have . . .

Lovely fluffy kittens
Babies wearing mittens
Both so sweet from angels up on high
So pure not knowing what may come by.

Ashleigh Sharif (12)
The Canterbuy High School, Canterbury

The Magic Box
(Based on 'Magic Box' by Kit Wright)

I will put in my box . . .
the purest blood of a unicorn,
shavings of magic white gold,
the buzzing of a bee
and the love of a happy family

I will put in my box . . .
the energy of a young child,
the crackling of a log fire

I will put in my box . . .
the spark of a live snake,
the untouched pure milk intended for a newborn baby,
the fruit from a tropical island,
the last leaf from the tree of knowledge.

Finally, I will place gently in my box,
A pure white snowflake falling from the sky on a summer's day.

The hinges on my box will be cast from the joints of an old man and the bolts on the box will be made from the most unblemished diamonds from the mines of South Africa.

Harry Turner (11)
The Canterbuy High School, Canterbury

The Highwayman

One time on a dark and windy night,
Some soldiers came marching by.
They looked up to see the stars
shining bright.
To be here they will cheat,
steel and lie.
Every night they sit there, frightened.
They're lucky to be alive.

Shannon Harris (12)
The Canterbuy High School, Canterbury

Sherbert Lemon Poem

I'm yellow and sweet,
And good to eat,
I'm sticky and hard,
When you crunch me, be on your guard!

Buy me in a shop,
My sourness makes you pop!
I come in a plastic bag,
Undoing me makes you mad!

In the middle
I'm wild
And it hurts when you bite,
Don't eat me at night,
Or your dentist will be in for a fright!
And so will you!

Johanna Barrett (11)
The Canterbuy High School, Canterbury

Holidays Are Here

H olidays are here!
O ff for Christmas and New Year
L oving every minute, holidays are great
I think this year's holidays came a bit late
D oughnuts, ice cream, popcorn, the lot
A t school all you get is slime in a pot
Y es at last the holidays are here!

Shane Scott (12)
The Canterbuy High School, Canterbury

Magic Box
(Based on 'Magic Box' by Kit Wright)

I will put in my box . . .
An angel wearing yellow with a sparkling hat,
A devil with glowing teeth.

I will put in my box . . .
A white horse with clippy-cloppy feet
A frog swimming in the sea
A boat flowing by.

I will put in my box . . .
A Chinese dragon breathing flames out of the sky
A yellow sun shining in my face.

I will put in my box . . .
A miaowing cat at my door

My box is made out of tinsel
Sparkling stars.

Stacie Macnally (12)
The Canterbuy High School, Canterbury

Winter Poem

W ind blowing in your hair
I ce on the floor so you slip over
N ice snow at Christmas time
T orrential rain
E arly nights
R emember the summer.

Kimberly Boden (12)
The Canterbuy High School, Canterbury

A Winter Poem

Winter is here,
The old men sit in the pub
Drinking their white, frothy beer.
I hate this part of year, cos it's so cold,
The people on the weather, said it was going to be cold,
Well that's what they told,
So it's the beginning of winter,
My lips are chapped and feel so bitter.

Jay Bennett (11)
The Canterbuy High School, Canterbury

The Beaten Boy

Through my telescope I am
seeing a crowded street
where people sleep

In the street I can see
a poor harmless boy
who's cold

The boy sits in the street
cold, cut and bruised and always
thinks about the same thing

His tears fall like a waterfall
in a hot country and he thinks about
how he was treated and when he
was beaten.

Nathan Procter (11)
The Canterbuy High School, Canterbury

The Magic Box
(Based on 'Magic Box' by Kit Wright)

I will put in my box . . .
A swift angel singing
A devil wearing white and a halo
An angel in red and with a pitchfork
A barking bellowing rotten-breathed dog

I will put in my box . . .
A flying fudge-filled football
A book with bulging pages
A beautiful newborn rabbit
The horns of a unicorn

I will put in my box . . .
The sweet smell of roses
The gentle breeze of flowing trees
A swift eagle flying
A nice fry-up for the morning
A beautiful bear growling

My box will look like the beginning of a mysterious
Adventure turning out to be the middle of nowhere,
The sun blazing down and a rainbow beating through.

Chloe Jackson (11)
The Canterbuy High School, Canterbury

In My Box
(Based on 'Magic Box' by Kit Wright

I will put in my box . . .
Every bark of a friendly dog, the sea crashing
against the wall. The screeching of a pencil
touching the paper.

I will put in my box . . .
The beautiful wings of a swan.
The screaming of my brothers.
The cat barking and the dog miaowing.

I will put in my box . . .
Rabbits running across the countryside,
A famous dancer and singer performing together.

Clarissa Couzins (12)
The Canterbuy High School, Canterbury

Excitement

Excitement is . . . when you go for a holiday.
Excitement is . . . when you get a new baby sister or brother
Excitement is . . . waking up and finding yourself in Heaven.
Excitement is . . . when Santa Clause brings lots of presents to you.
Excitement is . . . when it starts to snow in summer.
Excitement is . . . when you fall in love at first sight.
Excitement is . . . when you see a long lost friend.
Excitement is . . . when your pet starts talking to you.
Excitement is . . . when Earth rotates up and down.
Excitement is . . . when there is no gravity on Earth and we start flying in the air.
Excitement is . . . when all the boys turn by magic into girls.
Excitement is . . . part of our life and it's everything.

Humera Ansari (12)
Woodfield Middle School, Redditch

I Saw . . .

I saw a girl with an Afro
I saw a whale with wings,
I saw a school with no rules,
I saw a book with no words,
I saw a sofa with nitrous,
I saw an opera with drums,
I saw a nice teacher,
I saw a fun school.
I saw a playground with no children,
I saw a human with one eye.
I've seen a lot of things,
But there is nothing like this poem.

Jack Watton (12)
Woodfield Middle School, Redditch

Happiness Is . . .

Happiness is going to a theme park,
Happiness is not going to school.
Happiness is going to the cinema or Mega Bowl
Happiness is buying what you like when you go shopping.
Happiness is going to town with your friends.
Happiness is going on holiday.
Happiness is going out every day.

Raveena Haseeb (12)
Woodfield Middle School, Redditch

Stupidity

Stupidity is where you poke yourself in the eye
Stupidity is where you run into a lamp post
Stupidity is where you go to school on a Sunday
Stupidity is where you fall over a rock
Stupidity is where you fall out of the window
Stupidity is where you lob eggs at your own house.
Stupidity is where you read the dictionary
Stupidity is where you sit on the sofa instead of the toilet
Stupidity is where you throw a drink away but you need to drink it
Stupidity is picking your nose then scratching your head
Stupidity is where you're confused about a book
Stupidity is where you lob a brick at a window and ask for it back
Stupidity is where you forget your birthday
Stupidity is where you look in the mirror and ask yourself out.
Stupidity is me. Hold on!
Stupidity is forgetting your name
Stupidity is where you arrest yourself
Stupidity is skiving home time
Stupidity is where you try to jump off the Earth!
Stupidity is basically being stupid.

Matthew Knight (12)
Woodfield Middle School, Redditch

Four Seasons

The winter winds whirl around me,
The cold weather makes me shiver.
Snow is falling all around,
Winter, winter, go away.

Spring arrives so let's enjoy it,
Leaves are sprouting all around.
Grass is growing, green and bright.

The summer sun shines brightly above,
The hot sun warms my skin.
Shall I sunbathe on the beach?
Enjoy the warmth, whilst it lasts!

Summer's passed, autumn's forth,
Yellow leaves fall to the ground.
Find the scrunched up leaves lying there.

Stacey Cowley (11)
Woodfield Middle School, Redditch

The Fairy's Grace
(Inspired by 'A Midsummer Night's Dream' by William Shakespeare)

Fairy's singing a song of grace
While Titania's pretty face
Falls in deep sleep
Without knowing what comes next.

A head of an ass comes awake
Titania will be the bait,
When one's eye sets upon another
They will fall deeply in love with each other.

Titania awakes without knowing what comes next
When she thinks she has been blessed
Fairies prance around with the arrival of the future king
While they also dance and sing.

They finally rest for the rest of the night
When Titania finally has a fright
She finds an egg in her flowery bed
Meanwhile, the three couples are being wed.

Alex Oldnall (13)
Woodfield Middle School, Redditch

Puck
(Inspired by 'A Midsummer Night's Dream' by William Shakespeare)

I am mischievous, I do cause trouble
Tricking people to fall in love,
I never try to help
I just push and shove.

I am a good fairy, deep inside,
A heart that's made of gold.
I will gather all my pride,
And be good for all my life.

Abigail Dallaway (13)
Woodfield Middle School, Redditch

Zebra Confusion

The zebra is undoubtedly
A source of confusion
The alternate stripes
Is an optical illusion

Observing them is difficult
You easily lose track
Is it black upon white?
Or white upon black?

White men in Africa
Smoking their pipes
Think that a zebra is a
White horse with black stripes

Black men from Africa
Smoking different kinds of pipes
Know that a zebra
Is a black horse with white stripes.

Sam Oldnall (11)
Woodfield Middle School, Redditch

A Deserted School

It's the summer holidays
I'm in a deserted school,
There's just no way out
Nor no way in!
It's just too dark in here,
I'm scared.
The windows look like gloomy eyes,
Watching every little step of mine.
I can hear deep footsteps plodding
Along the darkened hallway,
The black coat looks like a ghost,
Getting ready to eat me, the closer
I approach!
I hide behind a little bin,
Which seems like it's gonna gobble me in!
The footsteps get closer, closer, closer
And so much closer, but suddenly,
'Hi Mohammed!'
It was Mr Bird all along!

Mohammed Soban (12)
Woodfield Middle School, Redditch

I'm Having A Dream

I'm having a dream
A very nice dream
I'm having a dream
About a golden stream.

In the stream, it's full of gold
The stream is also very, very cold.

When it rains
The stream flames and everyone
Gets into a big yellow crane.

I had a dream
A very nice dream
I had a dream
About a golden stream.

Jordan Taylor (12)
Woodfield Middle School, Redditch

Who Likes The Rain?

Who likes the rain?
I think it is a pain
It makes me insane
You can hide in a crane
To get out of the rain
It sprinkles down the windowpane
It makes curls in a lion's mane
When I am walking down the lane
Here it comes again and again.

Sherniece Pearson (12)
Woodfield Middle School, Redditch

A Year Of Adventure

Summer is toasted sizzling hot ground
Summer is the happiness of light, where fun and joy can begin.
Summer is where the flowers look at the sun to live,
Summer is the time to grow.
Summer is the time of happiness.

Autumn is when the leaves float and flutter to the ground,
Autumn is when the squirrels and animals collect food for winter.
Autumn is when the colours change in the day,
Autumn is between summer and winter.
Autumn is a great season.

Winter is the cold, frosty, chilly breeze on your skin,
Winter is the chilly wind, so everyone get inside.
Winter is when the animals hibernate and get cosy and warm.
Winter is sitting next to the crackling fire and falling asleep.
Winter is sugar dropping on your tongue and having a sweet, cold
and sharp taste.

Spring is the awakening of sun and the Earth,
Spring is the beginning of new life.
Spring comes with its new fresh scents.
Spring brings the birds out to sing,
Spring says goodbye to dark days and hello to
A year of adventure.

Raymond Stevens (11)
Woodfield Middle School, Redditch

Summer

S pring, spring bouncing
U p and down,
M ini creatures being found.
M ost people having fun in the sun
E xcept those in Australia.
R eason is, it's winter there!

Nabeela Khan (12)
Woodfield Middle School, Redditch

What Is A Poem?

A poem is a bundle of laughter
A poem is sad and funny
A poem is all about feelings
A poem is full of ideas
A poem is made up of emotions
A poem is similes and metaphors
A poem is a poem.

Stephanie Whitworth (11)
Woodfield Middle School, Redditch

What Is A Poem?

A poem is an emotion,
Happiness, anger and sadness.

A poem is a thought,
Feelings deep inside.

A poem is a river of imagination,
Thoughts and feelings deep inside.

A poem is a book,
Full of fantasy.

A poem is a cloud of ideas,
A poem is a storm of images.

Gemma Grubb (12)
Woodfield Middle School, Redditch

All Seasons

The sun shines all day long,
Lying on the beach
Ice cream melting in your hands
The sun out of reach

Leaves crunching under your feet
No flowers around
People cold, might be freezing
Mostly everything on the ground

Flowers out, bluebells out
Children singing songs of joy
Families going on holiday

Leaves coming off the trees
It's starting to get cold
Little children not playing out
Old men going bald.

Rochelle Parchment (12)
Woodfield Middle School, Redditch

Tell Me The Truth About Love!

Lovebirds just sit there happily and are friendly
to one another and trust each other.

Magically they appear, children,
adorable, funny children.

Mother's Day arrives,
flowers and chocolates are bought.

That family of love stays in their hearts
forever.

Sophie Hartles (12)
Woodfield Middle School, Redditch

What's In The Box?

Open up the box, what do you see?
Maybe some pictures, big and small,
The people in them jumping out of them one by one.

Open up the box, what do you see?
Maybe there's tiny people in a tiny village,
In their tiny world.

Open up the box, what do you see?
Maybe there are tiny people, in a tiny village,
In their tiny world.

Open up the box, what do you see?
Maybe there are angels, guarding us
With their big white wings spread in Heaven.

Open up the box, what do you see?
Maybe there's nothingness, invisible in the air,
Spread everywhere.

Rimah Rafiq (12)
Woodfield Middle School, Redditch

Tell Me The Truth About Love

Love is great, love is not
Some people think they are hot
Love is hard to explain
Even if your name is Jane

How about a nice slow dance
It could just be your last chance
What about a kiss or two
I have bought a present for you.

Matthew Ivory (12)
Woodfield Middle School, Redditch

I Predict A Riot

One glorious boggy day
Very wet day
Two teams collide
Baggies V Villa
As a defeat to a team
Villa lose
Brings hatred between them both
Lots of bad language
Then the leader shouts, 'Charge!'
One fan shouts, 'Get them!'
As they get out swords and daggers
Programmes and pencils
Then charge with anger
Football fans angry
As they start a bloody fight
A riot
Shouting and screams occur
Language and shouting
As another army comes to join
The coppers.

James Reffin, Ryan McIlravey, Casey Truman & Matthew Ivory (12)
Woodfield Middle School, Redditch

Tell Me The Truth About . . .

Is *love* a special thing,
Or is it in your love's kiss?
Does it make you wonder
What life might bring you?

Is *love* the real thing,
Or is it just another reason for Valentine's Day
And anniversaries?
If you had the chance to say those three special words
Would you say them
And make sure it's true?

No one knows what *love* is,
It always has more than one side,
Happy that they're there?
Sad because they've gone?
Angry because they broke your heart?
Love has different meanings
Some make you smile,
Put you in pain or make you cry.
But *love* cannot help itself.

Sarah Taylor (11)
Woodfield Middle School, Redditch

What Am I?

Me and you are quite often around,
Apart from when in the house,
Walking around until I die
And then getting chucked in the dustbin.
I go to get you and you're not there,
I go to Mum, 'Why aren't they there?'
She says, 'They're too small,
I'll get some more.'
But I want them back,
I go to the bin and get them out,
Squeeze my feet in until they pop out.
What are they?

Emma Flatley (12)
Woodfield Middle School, Redditch

Tell Me The Truth About Love

The truth about love is . . .
It's lovingly magical,
It is like stepping into a mystical world.

The thing about love is . . .
People say that it is gross and disgusting.

The point about love is . . .
That you feel loved
They say you look beautiful.

The best thing about love is . . .
Boys will stay and care for you
And say you look adorable and cuddly.

If you want to know about love . . .
Ask Mom, she will say it is nothing to be afraid of
Ask Dad, he will say you have got yourself a lad.

The last thing about love is . . .
When you have got yourself a lad
They will always make your day.

Coral Bruton (12)
Woodfield Middle School, Redditch

Tell Me The Truth About Love

Tell me the truth about love, tell me the truth about love.
Is it when you're feeling happy? Is it when you're feeling sad?
Is it when you're feeling angry? Is it when you're feeling glad?

Tell me the truth about love, tell me the truth about love.
Is it love when we're together? Is it love when we're apart?
Is it when we went out on our first date or when you broke my heart?

Tell me the truth about love, tell me the truth about love.
Is it when we have hugs? Is it when we have kisses?
Is it when you ask the question, 'Will you be my Mrs?'

Tell me the truth about love, tell me the truth about love.
Is it all of these things that are above?

Francine Walters (12)
Woodfield Middle School, Redditch

Open Up The Box

Open up the box, what do you see?
A dark space for ghouls to hang out,
Creepy-crawlies running with fear,
It's a dark and damp environment,
That only the wanted awaits.
It's no place for little children
As they disappear without a trace.

Paige Maoudis (12)
Woodfield Middle School, Redditch

Personification

This cage holds sadness
The tears like salty water
He is the blue-skinned
He is very cold
With very shaky hands
And long toenails
His eyes drooping like a wet dog
He cries like a lonely person
But people give him comfort.

This cage holds happiness
The laughing of his mouth
The shouting to get people's attention
She loves people's love
She goes to get some food to eat
The people give her presents
She is so joyful
But very happy with herself.

Thomas Fletcher (12)
Woodfield Middle School, Redditch

Superman

Superman is my hero
his heart rate never drops down to zero.

He saves people's lives
Superman is my kind of hero
he drops everything, even Lois
to help them out.

He works as a journalist
and joins the local press for a review.
When he hears screams for *'Superman!'*
he drops everything
to save lives.

That's my kind of hero
he could be yours too.
Out of the thousands out there
my hero is Superman
who's yours?

Chrissie Givans (11)
Woodfield Middle School, Redditch

Stations Of The Cross

I satisfied the crowd
The chosen way of death
My wounds were deep and painful
But this was only death.

Helpfulness and devotion
Made this god give me death.
I was whipped down to bone
A simple way of death.

My crown made of thorns
Helping towards my death
I carried my wooden cross
To my place of death.

Nails into my body
Bleeding towards death
People whispered and laughed
It wasn't long before death.

I questioned God
Why He wanted death
God never answered
It was finally death.

Lauren Poole (13)
Woodfield Middle School, Redditch

Stations Of The Cross

The moment of pain over and over again
the rush of blood spills out like a flood.
The iron touches the bare bone
as he is upright buried into stone.
The time has come, the end is near
but Jesus shows no pain or fear.
The King of Jews rest in peace
to come back one day and be free.

Jack Stevens (13)
Woodfield Middle School, Redditch

Jesus' Pain

Bone-tipped leather slashing at your back,
Ripping out your flesh with a mighty whack.
Stinging like a million angry bees,
In goes the vinegar, you're collapsing on your knees.
Crying and screaming as you carry the splintery cross,
Up the rough hill, digging in your wounds, too much blood loss.
Now you're at the top, your wrists and ankles are nailed,
To the high cross and your life is being failed.
You're hoisted up next to a murderer and thief,
Every time you breathe, you moan and heave.
It's turning to night and you can't carry on,
It's too much to bear, you shout, 'God where have you gone?'
Your eyes are blacking out, your head spinning,
Now you're dead and bad people are winning.

Katie Spencer (13)
Woodfield Middle School, Redditch

Poem

My life is colourful

I need a family

I want to have fun

Independence is won

Outgoing is what I like to be

Friends are the key to happiness

Honesty is my goal

I am confident

Ambition takes you places

Love makes the world turn.

Hester Phillips
Wycombe High School for Girls, High Wycombe

Things I Treasure . . . !

My *independence* makes me who I am, it makes Louisa . . . Louisa!

Risk is my real life truth or dare game . . . a sense of danger.

Family is what runs in my blood . . . that flows through my heart.

Freedom is the time when I have no barriers and when nothing is holding me back in my own little world.

Attention is my private theatre . . . with an exclusive audience . . . a stage for me to stand solo on . . . and a blinding spotlight gleaming on me . . . of course.

Performance is my one moment to amaze . . . a personal standing ovation.

Love keeps me strong . . . and it motivates my heart.

Friendship is what brings me up when I am down, that keeps a smile upon my face.

Senses are the five things which I live for.

Confidence is my mountain . . . bigger . . . taller than the other mountains and yet you will find me dancing about on the top.

Louisa Connolly Burnham (14)
Wycombe High School for Girls, High Wycombe

Shakespearean Sonnet

You are always here sitting on my mind
I think I know you are my true love
Whenever I am lost, me you will find
I feel inside, my heart you have removed
When you kiss me true you leave your soft mark
The gasping breath inside, my lungs are shaken
Our loving will survive the toughest bark
In marriage my fair hand you have taken
The redness like roses, my blushing cheeks
Through the darkening night you seem to come
Killing me softly are the long slow weeks
When you depart, it leads me to my doom
Our love, you and I have made shown and proved
The world now knows what it is to be loved.

Sophie Rowe & Laura Hylton (14)
Wycombe High School for Girls, High Wycombe

What Makes Me . . .

I refer to my friendship as eternal fire,
                family is the extended version of me,
independence is my self aspiration.

        I am not stupid, just intellectually challenged
        unique,   I am one in a million!

I am not dim but only colourful and bright, and it emphasises every part of me.
        Courageous is what I have chosen to become,
Imaginative and gifted with the ability to escape somewhere else

I am
    not of plastic,
        I am only but real
                and my happiness and joy is preserved!

Chevron Peters
Wycombe High School for Girls, High Wycombe

Untitled

Laughter makes you feel good inside and out
Being part of a family is a bond that no one else can break
To trust someone is to believe in them completely
When you love someone, everything looks good
Individuality is being different from the rest
Happiness is being content with who you are and what you are.
Independence is having no control or influence
From others on my life
Freedom is life with no barriers
Friends tell you when you are wrong
And praise you when you are right.

Marina Smith (14)
Wycombe High School for Girls, High Wycombe

Preserving Me

The quiet breeze and soft scents of the countryside
                                  The calm thud of horses' hooves
and the love.
Fun,
    smiles,
        laughter
            that they will always bring you.

In the warmth of the sun and summer
I relax, I am calm,

I'm in comfort   because I know
my family will always be there
                just for me.

                My friends will always care,
will always dry any tears with a single smile.

I escape with music,
        covered   in
           my   own
             circle of trust
                protecting my world
            in a way only I can.
        Preserving the world which makes me, me.

Ella Blakstad (13)
Wycombe High School for Girls, High Wycombe

Worthwhile

Drama can be all consuming

                              Like *laughter* can be enveloping.

Writing captures the emotions
that you feel, even the ones that
you can't talk about

                              with *family*, though you know they
                                        are always behind you.

Just as *friends* are the wings
you need to help you fly.

                                      As *freedom* is kept alive
                                      by our inner strengths,

Films unlock the door to
another's reality and

                        Books can transport you to other
                              worlds; escape routes when
                                      times are tough.

But *love;* love is what makes it
all worthwhile.

Holly Hewlett (14)
Wycombe High School for Girls, High Wycombe

Unique

Unique
    It's what makes you love me!
        Family is what brings the ups and downs in life
Love is beautiful and cannot be matched!
        Friends are forever and should not be lost!
            Happiness is when I smile around you!
Trust is the root of everything!
        Respect is what makes me love you
            Laughter is what makes my life worth living!

Nikki Benyon
Wycombe High School for Girls, High Wycombe

Me

Tip-top is always loving and caring
                Knowledge keeps me going
Quiet helps me stop and think
                Life brings me back
Books help me fly
                Precious is seventeen
Freedom is precious too
                We are always together
My family in my heart
                Even when I am alone.

Femke Hyman
Wycombe High School for Girls, High Wycombe

Our World

Underwater beauty and nature are both wonders,
        but the greatest wonder of the world is friendship
and happiness too,
        all taking part in the tapestry of life
and trust is good as well but
        it is always worth questioning what's around you.
Everyone's love is
        unique
but everyone is the same
        in that our most unique love is that of your family.

Vicky Jewell (13)
Wycombe High School for Girls, High Wycombe

Life's Colours

Millions of colours being seen for the first time
                All over the world through the eyes of newborns
However, endless time ticks on
                And rivers keep on flowing
Until they meet waterfalls when the
                Peacefulness shatters into a roaring thunder
Tick-tock, on goes time
                The water becomes mist at the bottom
In a sudden creepy gentleness
                Like the ending of life.

Leanne Robinson (14)
Wycombe High School for Girls, High Wycombe

Life

        Life that is and life that was . . .
A feeling that's washed away
        In enchanted space and enchanted talk.
God is always all encompassing always.
        To have hope and have faith in life and God
And enchantment.
        To have friends that stay,
Family stays with you as well.
        To have the written word, a way to express love and feelings.
The light of rubies sparkling catches your eye and
        Makes you shine bright.

Diana Newman
Wycombe High School for Girls, High Wycombe

Villanelle

I just cannot get you out of my mind
I think that I may be falling in love
It's true happiness that I want to find
Your imprint on me I just can't remove
Onto me you really have left your mark
Whenever I see you I am shaken
Our names are now carved onto a tree bark
My beating heart from me you have taken
You left a kiss upon my blushing cheek
Every single day closer we become
I love you more every hour, day and week
When we are apart I fall into doom
So far to you my true love has been proved
A man just like you I have never loved.

Sanaa Aslam & Hester Phillips
Wycombe High School for Girls, High Wycombe

Lumpy

That's my cute little Heffalump,
Small and fat and proud of that,
Running through trees with a skip and a jump.

Trips over his feet and falls with a bump,
Thought it was time for a little something and sat,
That's my cute little Heffalump.

Clumsily climbing up a tree stump,
Searching for sweetness, the air he sniffs at,
Running through trees with a skip and a jump.

He spies a tree with honey in a lump,
Knocking on the trunk with a rat-a-tat-tat,
That's my cute little Heffalump.

Clambering up the tree with a jump, jump, jump,
Falls through the honey and that is that.
Running through trees with a skip and a jump.

Feeling quite sticky and with a sore rump,
Small and fat and quite proud of that,
That's my cute little Heffalump,
Running through the trees with a skip and a jump.

Beth Molyneux & Katie Hart
Wycombe High School for Girls, High Wycombe

Basketball Villanelle

Basketball is my favourite sport
It is a game that keeps me fit
I like the way they dribble up and down the court

A big orange ball I have bought
I feel sorry for those who on the bench sit
Basketball is my favourite sport

To keep myself going I eat McDonald's with a fork
Get in my way it is you I will hit
I like the way they dribble up and down the court

Before you can score, the ball you must have caught
Yellow and purple are the colours of our kit
Basketball is my favourite sport

Over the ball we have all fought
Annoy me and in your eye I will spit
I like the way they dribble up and down the court

To win the game is what we all sought
The whole court by burning lights is lit
Basketball is my favourite sport
I like the way they dribble up and down the court.

Ade, Abi, Natalie & Sabine
Wycombe High School for Girls, High Wycombe

My Bacon

Alert! Alert! My food has been taken.
Oh, it smells so good,
And, I don't even like bacon.

I bet it was her, that sister of mine, for goodness sake.
And now with her I'm in a mood.
Alert! Alert! My food has been taken.

I shouldn't really care so much, but all that's left in the fridge
                                        is an empty beer can.
But I hate it when she takes my food,
And, I don't even like bacon.

And I called to Mum to find the cracken*
And discover she's gone to the woods.
Alert! Alert! My food has been taken.

Although to be angry was not my intention.
But she shouldn't have been so rude,
And I don't even like bacon.

On her return, she apologises with determination.
So now she's alright, she's kind of a dude.
Alert! Alert! My food has been taken,
And I don't even like bacon.

Cracken - a deep sea monster.

Lucy West (14) & Diana Newman
Wycombe High School for Girls, High Wycombe

The Bonding Of Honest Minds

Friendship is the bonding of honest minds
It's filled with loyalty, laughter and love.
And being together one often finds
That even the fighting cannot remove
The loving and kindness that leaves a mark
Even if your whole world has been shaken
Our friendship will survive like toughest bark.
Though two different roads we may have taken
I smile when I think of your rosy cheeks,
And even though the afterlife soon comes
I will always look fondly on these years
When we felt so far away from all the doom.
And so it is you, my friend, who has prov'd,
That above all other things, I have lov'd.

Ella Blakstad (13) & Holly Hewlett (14)
Wycombe High School for Girls, High Wycombe

Villanelle

'Quick after that man!
He is still in sight
He's stolen my jam!'

The little old lady Pam
Was looking for a daring fight
'Quick after that man!'

She jumped on her scooter, *bam!*
She went as fast as the speed of light
'He has stolen my jam!'

She rode over a lamb
The man turned white
'Quick after that man!'

She took out her snappy cam
But the man turned a sharp right
'He has stolen my jam!'

The lady cursed, 'Damn!'
In a helicopter he took flight
'Quick after that man!
He has stolen my jam!'

Sophie Rowe, Harriet Gwilt & Laura Hylton (14)
Wycombe High School for Girls, High Wycombe

Expressing Myself

Expressing myself in my own way and
By writing,
   I am discovering what's
               in my imagination.
               I'm learning all the time
in more ways than one.
            I'm bubbling with
emotion and love,
           all of it genuine.
        I am
what you see.
        I am
the real
        Natalie Cregan.

Natalie Cregan
Wycombe High School for Girls, High Wycombe

Untitled

Faith is a vision of things concealed, sounds of things not heard,
Thinking provokes pondering and challenges faith,
Love is the art of selflessness and warms hearts,
Laughter is the art of fun and warms minds,
Imagination is charmed to create a thrilling reality,
Risk is taken but illusion keeps us untouchable,
Creativity allows us to explore our imagination,
Expression leads us to make a mark of individuality,
Freedom should be enchanting, it has remarkable value,
Friendship embraces us for always, strives to keep us laughing.

Katie Hart
Wycombe High School for Girls, High Wycombe